HISTORY
CARVED IN STONE

A GUIDE TO THE ARCHAEOLOGICAL PARK OF THE RUINS OF COPAN

Fourth Edition

William L. Fash and Ricardo Agurcia Fasquelle

Illustrations by Barbara W. Fash
Photographs by David Beyl
Maps by Carlos Gastelum

Asociación Copán
Copán Ruinas, Honduras

In its first edition,
we dedicated this guide
to Doña Cristiana Nufio de Figueroa,
whose faith in our work over the years
made it possible.

We would like to dedicate
this fourth edition
to Don Jorge Bueso Arias
whose leadership and unwavering support has
been a bastion of strength
to the Copan Association.

ASOCIACION
COPAN

PUBLICADO POR  EDITORIAL TRANSAMÉRICA, S.A.
Honduras

ISBN: 978-99926-722-2-8

Copyright Asociación Copán, 2007
Copyright photographs: David Beyl
Copyright illustrations: Barbara Fash

TABLE OF CONTENTS

INTRODUCTION   6

8   Previous Interpretations of Ancient Maya Society
10   Contemporary Perspectives

THE ARCHAEOLOGICAL PARK   12

General Description

15   The City and its Wards
16   The Principal Group
17   The Great Plaza
23   The Acropolis
24   The West Court
27   The East Court
30   Tunnels
31   Rosalila
34   Sub-Jaguar Tunnel

ARCHAEOLOGY AND HISTORY
AT COPAN   36

36   Monuments and Rulers
37   Altar Q and the Late Rulers
38   Copan's Dynasty
40   Dates of Inscribed Monuments
47   Earlier Rulers
51   Recent Archaeological Investigations
54   Las Sepulturas
59   The Principal Group
62   The Collapse

64   BIBLIOGRAPHY

INTRODUCTION

This guidebook serves those visitors to Copan who wish to understand the significance of this ancient city, without expecting to become experts on the subject; it aspires to be an easy reference for the layperson. In it we have tried to highlight the most recent theories, research and discoveries.

The land of the Maya consists of approximately 324,000 square kilometers in what are now the western parts of Honduras and El Salvador, all of Guatemala and Belize, and the southern Mexican states of Chiapas, Tabasco, Campeche, Yucatán, and Quintana Roo. In this same territory, there are presently about 6 million people who speak one of the 28 Mayan languages still in use. They are the direct descendants of the ancient Maya.

LAND OF THE MAYA

ATLANTIC OCEAN

AN SEA

The Classic Period dates from 250 to 900 A.D. and is thought of as the "golden age" of Pre-Columbian Maya civilization. It is the main subject of this guide. During this time around 60 principal kingdoms were formed in the Maya area, each one controlling an area of about 2,500 square kilometers. These centers and the areas between them were home to a population of two to three million people, curiously, a much smaller number than today.

At certain times, these kingdoms were united into larger political entities called "regional states", which had their seats in the principal centers of the Maya world: Calakmul, Caracol, Cobá, Copan, Naranjo, Palenque, Piedras Negras, Tikal, Uxmal, Yaxchilán and Chichén Itzá. The territory for some of these states could have been as large as 30,000 square kilometers.

Traditionally, Tikal has been considered the largest of these cities, with its central area covering an expanse of some 123 square kilometers, sustaining a population of about 62,000 people. For its part, the 24 square kilometers surrounding the center of Copan sustained a population of about 21,000, with the greater kingdom serving as home to an additional 7,000 citizens. Although small on this scale, Copan was superbly advanced in many arts, and particularly in stone carving, which is why it wins the hearts of visitors. If Tikal was like New York, Copan was like Paris.

Previous Interpretations of Ancient Maya Society

The discoveries of recent archaeological projects in Copan as well as the advances in archaeology in general have obliged us to re-evaluate the conclusions of previous generations of investigators regarding Copan and the ancient Maya society.

In the traditional view, ancient Maya society was conceived of as a theocracy built around a priestly class. The architectural complex of the ruins, especially in the area of the pyramids, was considered to be exclusively a ceremonial center, filled with temples. Copan was not considered an urban center; it was thought that only the priests resided there, while the vast majority of the population lived in small hamlets dispersed in the countryside. Only on periodic ceremonial occasions did the people congregate in the plazas of the Principal Group.

These early scholars believed that the personages depicted in the art were none other than the gods themselves, or the priests; there was no consideration that they might represent historical individuals. In the same way, the hieroglyphic writing was thought to reflect a system of prophecy by which the priests documented their predictions of events based on astrological observations. There was no place for the idea that the Maya hieroglyphic writing system, like their art, contained historical data about kings and nobles who played the leading roles in Maya society. Likewise, it was assumed that war had not played an important role in this Classic society, thus the notion that it was a peaceful theocracy.

SCULPTED MACAW ON THE BALLCOURT

9

Contemporary Perspectives

The modern age of archaeology in Copan began in 1975 with the Copan Valley Project of the Peabody Museum of Harvard University. Almost a hundred years earlier (1891-1895), this same institution captured the attention of the scientific world with its discoveries, giving Copan the illustrious place that it was to retain in studies of the ancient Maya.

Likewise, beginning in 1977, the Government of Honduras, through the then Ministry of Culture and Tourism and its agencies, the Honduran Institute of Tourism and the Honduran Institute of Anthropology and History, gave continuity to this tradition with a series of projects which have continued to the present and whose results have gone much farther than anyone anticipated.

The investigations of these projects—carried out by prominent scientists and humanists from many countries—pursue a wide array of interests, including studies of physical and social anthropology, ethnohistory, ecology, art, writing, and especially archaeology, through intensive excavations in the Acropolis, Great Plaza, Las Sepulturas and El Bosque, and the mapping and testing of thousands of smaller ruins throughout the valley.

STELAE AND ALTARS IN THE GREAT PLAZA

These investigations have permitted scholars, for the first time, to reconstruct in significant detail the development of the ancient city through time, to discern the historical forces at work and to begin to understand the personalities that helped shape the destiny of this remarkable ancient city, giving us a new vision of the Maya world.

Among the recent investigations, perhaps the most informative have been the studies on the hieroglyphs. It has been demonstrated that the hieroglyphic texts of

HIEROGLYPHIC TEXT ON ALTAR V

Copan, though firmly anchored in calendrical and astronomical calculations, actually refer to the life and times of the Maya rulers and the nobles who made up their royal courts. Moreover, it is now clear that the persons depicted on the stelae (monolithic stone statues) of Copan are those very rulers.

This interpretation is more in keeping with what we know of other ancient civilizations, such as that of Egypt, where the majority of the art was dedicated to the aggrandizement of the pharaohs and their families. Events such as the birth, accession to the throne, important battles and conquests, rituals, anniversaries of earlier events, and the death of the rulers can now be deciphered on the stelae, altars, and other hieroglyphic sculptures of Copan. Many texts contain long historical narratives, sometimes even including the name of the monuments on which they were inscribed. In some archaeological sites scholars have even been able to decipher the name of the artists who created and signed these great works of art. Likewise, experts are finding more evidence to support the thesis that the texts were written in an ancestral language closely related to the Cholan linguistic group which includes the Chortí, Mayan language which is still spoken in the vicinity of Copan.

THE
ARCHAEOLOGICAL
PARK

At present, more than 160,000 people from over 60 countries arrive in the Copan Valley on an annual basis for the purpose of visiting this majestic ancient Maya metropolis. The
Government of Honduras declared the Archaeological Park a
National Monument in 1982. The legislation passed encompasses the entire Copan River Valley in order to protect not just
the urban nucleus of the prehispanic city but also its tributary
communities, with which it formed a single sociopolitical unit.

The Honduran Institute of Anthropology and History (IHAH)
is in charge of administering this national monument. At the
international level, UNESCO declared Copan a World Heritage
Site in 1980 principally because of the Hieroglyphic Stairway,
giving it its well deserved place with the most distinguished cultural monuments of the world.

Scientists concerned with the conservation of the site have
studied the deterioration of the stone used for sculptures and
masonry buildings. They have all concluded that the greatest
damage comes from drastic variations in temperature and
humidity (often occurring within the same day), torrential rains,
and ground moisture. All of these cause a weakening of the
surface structure of the stones, resulting in the flaking off of the
surface. This process, called exfoliation is particularly evident
on the bases of the Copan stelae and altars. For this reason,
some of the monuments of the Park have been roofed.
Professionals have proceeded to make exact replicas of some of

these delicate sculptures in order to move the originals to the Sculpture Museum where they can be better cared for. In the field, these replicas can be exhibited without roofing, preserving a more traditional environment at the archaeological site.

General Description

Considered the "Athens of the New World" by the famous Maya archaeologist Sylvanus Morley, the Ruins of Copan represent one of the most spectacular cultural achievements of the ancient world. As such, the ruins have been the focus of numerous expeditions of exploration and investigation, beginning in the 1830s and still ongoing.

Copan occupies the premier position among Maya sites as far as the quality and quantity of stone sculptures is concerned, including stelae and altars. It also has the privilege of having the longest inscribed text in the New World, in the Hieroglyphic Stairway of Structure 10L-26. Additionally, thousands of fragments of architectural sculpture formed striking decorative

1. THE GREAT PLAZA   2. THE ACROPOLIS   3. EL BOSQUE

mosaic designs on the façades of the buildings of the ancient city. Most of the best examples of these can be admired in the Sculpture Museum.

The City and its Wards

The urban nucleus of Copan is composed of the Principal Group, which was the political, civic, and religious center, and a series of residential neighborhoods surrounding it. The modern Archaeological Park includes two of these wards, which are connected by causeways (called "sacbe" or "white road" in Mayan) to the Principal Group. One of these is located to the southwest and is called "El Bosque", while the other, to the northeast, is "Las Sepulturas".

4. LAS SEPULTURAS

In the 24 square kilometers immediately surrounding the Principal Group, the remnants of 3,450 buildings have been registered. More than one thousand of these define the urban nucleus of the city, which incorporates the wards of El Bosque and Las Sepulturas in an area of approximately 2.1 square kilometers. Based on the study of these buildings, it has been estimated that the overall population of Copan, at its greatest height in the eighth century and including its rural areas came to more than 28,000 inhabitants.

The Principal Group

1. THE GREAT PLAZA   2. THE ACROPOLIS

The Principal Group encompasses a forested area of 12 hectares and is composed of the Great Plaza and the Acropolis. Both may be subdivided into smaller architectural elements, consisting of rectangular courtyards (patios or plazas) surrounded by pyramidal platforms with buildings on top. Both the Great Plaza and the Acropolis reflect enormous amounts of labor: the former for its great size (more than three hectares of leveled and paved surfaces) and the second due to its enormous, elevated mass (rising more than 30 meters or 100 feet above the valley floor). The term "Acropolis" ("city on a hill") was another concept borrowed from Athens by early Maya scholars, but in the case of Copan the "hill" is entirely man-made. The Acropolis comprises the succession of palaces, temples, and administrative buildings constructed for and used by Copan's rulers and their royal courts over a span of four centuries, from about AD 400 until not long after AD 800.

Most of the buildings in the Principal Group were profusely adorned with stone sculpture. Copan has the most elaborate development of this art form of any Maya city. In turn, this sculpture has allowed experts to gain a unique insight into the meaning that the ancient Maya attributed to their massive architecture: they built a symbolic landscape that mimicked and enhanced the natural one. The giant pyramidal platforms were seen as sacred mountains (witz). The entrances to the temples on top of these were held as sacred caves, portals to the underworld. The plazas in front of them represented the flat surfaces of valleys or, alternately, still bodies of water like lakes, ponds or lagoons.

In these plazas the Maya would control the flow of water, so that during the rainy season (June through November) they could flood these at will. This water management system was facilitated by the paving of the courtyards with thick layers of lime plaster (stucco) which created an impermeable and uniform surface. During major rainstorms parts of the Great Plaza can still be seen transforming themselves into a lagoon.

The Great Plaza

1. SUN COURT   2. STRUCTURE 4   3. COURT OF HIEROGLYPHIC STAIRWAY
4. BALLCOURT   5. TEMPLE 26   6. TEMPLE 11

The Great Plaza consists of large, open spaces. It is also the confluence of the two main causeways of the city. It is evident that it served for public events having the capacity to hold thousands of people. At its northern end, the Great Plaza is framed on three sides by elongated steps that served as seats for the multitudes and formed the Sun Court. Built for the most part in the 8th century by the 13th Ruler, Waxaklajun Ub'ah K'awil (18 Rabbit), the center of this open-air theater boasts seven stelae and eleven altars, forming one of the most beautiful sculpture gardens of Copan. This served as a stage for ritual acts of enormous social importance, principal among these were rites associated with the worship of the Sun God, K'inich Ahau.

STELA H

Recent research by Honduran scholars from the National University of Honduras (UNAH) has shown that in the Sun Court both the placement of the sculpted monuments (stelae and altars) as well as that of the architecture (including the staircases) were designed to facilitate solar observation throughout the year. Three events, each of which repeats twice annually, were of particular importance here. These were the solstices, equinoxes and zenith passages. Although the festivities and ceremonies would have lasted for days, the culminating moments of observation occurred at dawn and dusk on those days.

The southern end of this Sun Court is defined by Structure 4, which is the radial pyramid with staircases on all its sides that is first seen as one walks from the Visitor's Center into the

SECTION OF SCULPTURE GARDEN, STRUCTURE 4 IN THE BACKGROUND

Principal Group. It was built by the 13th Ruler, but in its construction fill was found Stela 35, one of the earliest monuments from Copan dated to about AD 400. Like many other wonderful sculptures of this site, it was broken up and re-utilized by the ancient Maya. In this manner many beautiful works of art lent supernatural force from the sacred ancestors to the latest buildings. The unique position and form of Structure 4 argue for its having been part of the system of constructions commissioned by the 13th Ruler to facilitate astronomical and particularly solar observation in the Great Plaza.

At the southern end of the Great Plaza, in the Court of the Hieroglyphic Stairway, there is another theater with small bleachers on the North side and enormous stone benches going up to the Acropolis on the South, both overlooking the Great Ballcourt. It is evident that here the focus was on sports, a Mesoamerican tradition of enormous importance even today.

The Ballcourt's graceful playing alley is bordered by parallel buildings with large sloping benches ornately decorated with scarlet macaws. It was commissioned in its final form by the 13th Ruler of Copan at the end of his reign, in the year AD 738. We are not entirely certain as to how the game was played here, but we do now from

MACAW

BALLCOURT

19

the accounts of Spanish historians who witnessed the game in many parts of Mesoamerica, that it was played with a ball made of solid rubber. This made it very heavy so that the players could only hit it with their hips or thighs, over which they wore protection. In some scenes of Maya art, the bloody sacrifice of losing players is shown, although more common was the practice seen by the Spanish of the losers and their fans having to give up their jewelry and fine clothing.

The ballgame was also heavily imbued with cosmic and religious connotations. At Copan the macaw iconography is particularly associated with the sun and its movement across the heavens. With its bright yellow and red colors, and graceful flight overhead, the macaw was particularly well suited for this. The game ball itself was another symbol for the fiery sphere of the sky. Scenes coming from the three ballcourt markers at Copan (now in the Town Museum) have been associated with very important mythical narratives of creation from the Popol Vuh (sacred book of the Quiché Maya from the highlands of Guatemala). In this sacred book, the playing alley is also the stage through which communion could take place with the watery underworld where the ancestors reside.

Bordering the Great Ballcourt's southern end-zone is the majestic Temple 26 with its grandiose Hieroglyphic Stairway. Over two decades of recent work on this building have given us the most complete historical view of any single building at the site. In AD 755 it was inaugurated in its final form by the 15th Ruler of Copan, K'ak' Joplaj Chan K'awil ("Smoke Shell"), who is portrayed in front of the base of the stairs on Stela M. Its main theme was that of royal ancestor worship, embedded in the context of war and sacrifice. On the risers of its main stairway was carved the longest single hieroglyphic inscription of the ancient New World, narrating the official dynastic history of the city. The text was interspersed with the seated portraits of its protagonists, the Kings of ancient Copan, dressed in full warfare regalia. Recent research has shown that the original, shorter version of the Hieroglyphic Stairway adorned a now-buried earlier temple-pyramid. This original text was dedicated to the memory of the 12th Ruler, whose elaborate and richly stocked tomb was discovered inside the pyramid in 1989.

Inside Temple 26, still earlier constructions were found dating back to the founding of the city. Among these were some amazing monuments, including the Motmot floor marker (now at the Sculpture Museum), Stela 63,

CERAMIC EFFIGY FIGURE LIDS PORTRAY THE FIRST 12 RULERS OF COPAN.

the earliest stela at the site (also at the Sculpture Museum), and the Altar of the Papagayo Structure. The tomb of the 12th Ruler, Smoke Imix, whose longevity and achievements make him

INTERIOR OF PAPAGAYO STRUCTURE WITH ITS ALTAR AND STELA 63

21

arguably the most important one in the site's history, is the largest funerary chamber known in the city. The tomb's ceramic effigy figure lids portraying the first 12 rulers of Copan (now at the town museum) have become a hallmark for the site.

STELA N

The southern end of the Court of the Hieroglyphic Stairway is defined by the Acropolis, dominated here by the massive staircase of Temple 11, or Temple of the Inscriptions. At the base of it stands Stela N, one of the most delicately carved monuments of Copan. It is another portrait of the 15th Ruler and dates from the end of his reign in AD 761. Due west of the stela, in the Southwest corner of the court, we can see the only existing drain in this whole area, which when blocked turns the court into a lagoon.

STAIRCASE ON TEMPLE 11 (TEMPLE OF THE INSCRIPTIONS)

The Acropolis

1. THE WEST COURT   2. THE EAST COURT

In contrast to the Great Plaza, the Acropolis is a more private area, with restricted access and reduced spaces. This was the central precinct of political and religious power, the headquarters of the ruler and his court. Architecturally, the Acropolis is composed of two courtyards: the East Court, or Court of the Jaguars, and the West Court.

Access to the lofty summit is restricted by the very steep staircase that rises from the Court of the Hieroglyphic Stairway up to the Temple of the Inscriptions and another staircase at the northeast corner (now destroyed) that the early explorers Stephens and Catherwood reported in 1841. The other sides of the Acropolis are characterized by high terrace walls. Once on top of the platform circulation is further restricted by at least two walled gates, on the southern corners of Temple 16.

The two-storied exterior of Temple 11 (completed in AD 773) was adorned with a giant cosmogram that was the centerpiece of the southern end of the Great Plaza. The building's four entrances on the cardinal directions were elegantly decorated with extensive hieroglyphic texts heralding the accession to the throne by Copan's 16th Ruler, Yax Pasaj Chan Yoaat, in the year AD 763. The back side of Temple 11 overlooks the

23

West Court and has, on its lower section, an area known as the Reviewing Stand, which is discussed below.

The West Court

1. TEMPLE 11   2. TEMPLE 16   3. ALTAR Q

 The West Court is a symbolic sacred landscape marked by its sculpture as the watery underworld of the Maya cosmos. Among the sculptures easiest to identify for this purpose are two large shells resting on top of the main platform of the Reviewing Stand. Atop the neighboring Structure 13 there are also stone sculptures of two alligator heads. This is a place for the veneration of the royal ancestors, who, at the end of their lives, follow the sun to the west into the dark, aquatic, world of the dead.

The Reviewing Stand itself was a stage for the performance of rituals and sacrifices. The three markers that are placed in front of it mark it as a symbolic ballcourt, while the text that is on its steps reaffirms this.

Outlining the east side of the West Court and towering over the entire Acropolis is Temple 16. At the base of its 20 meter tall stairway is Altar Q, arguably the most important historical

24

monument of the site and one that, in keeping with the theme of the courtyard, emphasizes the veneration of the royal ancestors.

Like Temple 11, Altar Q and Temple 16 were commissioned by the 16th Ruler. Their dedication took place in the year AD 775. On the four sides of the square altar are represented all 16 monarchs of the dynasty. They are portrayed in their historical order and each is seated on a hieroglyph that spells out his name. On the front of the altar (west side), the last ruler Yax Pasaj symbolically receives the "staff of rulership" from the founder of the dynasty, K'inich Yax K'uk' Mo' (Great-Sun First Quetzal Macaw), and in so doing proclaims his legitimate authority. In the upper part of the altar, a long hieroglyphic text narrates important events associated with the arrival of the Founder at Copan and the establishment of his dynasty in the year AD 426. Toward the end it mentions the dedication of the "altar of K'inich Yax K'uk' Mo'" by Yax Pasaj in AD 775. The text is placed so that it could be read by someone standing on

the steps of Temple 16. Its narrative is so important that it was probably known by heart by most ancient residents and probably recited or chanted on many ceremonial occasions.

ALTAR Q FROM ABOVE

ALTAR Q: 16TH RULER RECEIVES STAFF FROM 1ST RULER

This inscription makes it evident that the Founder came from outside Copan and that his arrival was an act that transcended fifteen changes of government and survived for close to four hundred years at the forefront of rulership, something unparalleled at any other Maya site. The question of the origins of this great lord is the subject of considerable discussion among experts today. Excavations of the earliest archaeological levels under Temple 16 have found a tomb that it is believed to be his final resting place. The sequence of constructions at this site (including such famous buildings as Yehnal, Margarita and Rosalila), and their iconographic emphasis on the veneration of this ancestor lend considerable support to this conclusion.

Like Temple 26, Temple 16 is dedicated to warfare, sacrifice, and the veneration of royal ancestors. The main ancestor portrayed here is K'inich Yax K'uk' Mo', who is represented in many of the sculptures that adorned this building. Like Temple 11, this giant edifice had a two-storied tower built on its summit. This is an architectural feature that was probably borrowed by Yax Pasaj from the great Maya city of Palenque, on the westernmost edge of the Maya world, his mother's homeland.

 As the visitor walks around the southern edge of Temple 16, en route to the East Court, he overlooks a building compound known locally as El Cementerio. This was the royal residence of Yax Pasaj. It consists of a number of rectangular courtyards outlined by graceful buildings of stone blocks. This is where the king's wives and children ate, slept, played, and carried out their daily lives. The main courtyard is dominated by Structure 32 which was the ruler's house. It was once adorned with elaborate mosaic sculptures on its external façades, representing a young lord sitting on a water-lily monster. This was probably a portrait of Yax Pasaj and his supernatural companion, the rain god, Chak. A full-scale reconstruction of this lovely structure can be seen in the Sculpture Museum.

The East Court

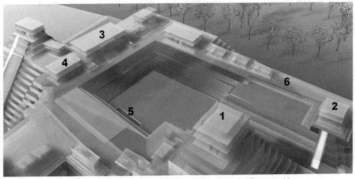

1. TEMPLE 16   2. TEMPLE 18   3. TEMPLE 22   4. POPOL NAH
5. JAGUAR SUN GOD   6. JAGUAR THRONE

Temple 18 on the southeastern corner of the Acropolis is the funerary temple of Yax Pasaj. On the delicate carvings of its wall panels, he is exalted as a great warrior. It seems that this ruler, again harking back to the ancestry of his mother, built his tomb underneath a temple with a central staircase leading to it, much in the same way that Pakal the Great, the most famous king of Palenque, did.

Unfortunately when this building was excavated and restored in the late 1970's, it was found that the burial chamber was empty. It had been disturbed in ancient times and it is quite possible that even though the last king of Copan was buried here, his body and its offerings were removed and taken elsewhere. The last stela of Copan, No. 11, with its portrait of a deceased Yax Pasaj in the underworld, was placed on the western side of this building.

Moving North from Temple 18 into the West Court, one follows the edge of the Archaeological Cut carved out by the Copan River in the past few centuries. Now destroyed, but seen by earlier explorers and researchers, were Structures 20 and 21. Based on their accounts and the sculpture fragments associated with these buildings, it is believed that the first of these was the "House of the Bats" while the second was the "House of Knives". Both are thought to be the work of the 13th Ruler.

According to the Popol Vuh, sacred book of the Quiche Maya, the House of the Bats is the place where sacrificial victims were held before being taken to partake in the rites that brought a tortuous end to their lives. The Copan example was a two-storied jailhouse decorated on its façades with intimidating killer bats (examples of these are found at both the Town Museum and the Sculpture Museum), dark denizens of the underworld.

The House of the Knives was decorated with knives and obsidian (volcanic glass). This could have implied that it was an abode for guards or warriors, or (following the Popol Vuh) that it was a place where knives were used for sacrifices.

Temple 22 closes off the North side of the East Court and dominates the entire compound. This building was commissioned by the 13th Ruler in AD 715 and is considered to have been the most beautiful one at Copan. It is eloquently marked on its corner masks as a "sacred mountain"; on its tall and ele-

TEMPLE 22

28

gant façade the young maize god was portrayed sprouting from the mountain; and on its principal doorway is carved a giant earth monster mouth, representing the entrance to a sacred cave, creating a ritual landscape where it is believed that royal bloodletting and sacrifice took place in honor of the deceased ancestors.

The elaborate sculpted throne (now in the Sculpture Museum) found in its interior chambers is one of the most exquisite works of art in the entire Maya area. (See photo on P. 60.) It consists of a cosmogram with the Underworld (marked by skulls) represented below the throne in its lower register; the Middle World where mortals reside and the king would stand or sit, framed by two sky bearers (Bacabs), in its middle register; and the Heavens in the upper register represented by a two-headed sky dragon whose undulating body closes the space over the throne. It was a place for regal ritual, where the king would exercise his religious duties framed by the symbols of the entire Maya cosmos.

Next to this magnificent temple is Structure 22-A. Identified as the "Popol Nah" it is the "Mat House" or "Community House" where the king would gather with his court and principal advi-

POPOL NAH

sors to hold council and make the principal decisions governing the state. It was built by the 14th Ruler, K'ak' Joplaj Chan K'awil, in the year AD 746. Directly in front of the Council House is a long dance platform, used in the feasts that followed the convening of the community leaders. Council houses are still in use among the Maya today, and the town of Copan has seen fit to construct its own example, as part of the Municipal Building.

Like the West Court, the East Court is also a sacred landscape, identified by its sculpture as a place of sun worship. On the East side of the courtyard a sculpture of the Sun God was once placed. It consists of a youthful portrait of this deity and symbolizes the rising sun, which would have come up behind it every day. On the opposite side of the court is its counterpart: a large portrait of the Jaguar Sun God of the Underworld. Here

JAGUAR SUN GOD

the setting sun is shown inside the open jaws of a large jaguar as he is being symbolically swallowed by the night. He himself is transforming into a jaguar (note his feline ears) as he prepares to wrestle with the real jaguars, who were the denizens of the night. Two such creatures are portrayed waiting for him on the staircase below.

In the middle of the courtyard are three stone markers. Like those in front of the Reviewing Stand, they mark the site as a symbolic ballcourt and, as such, as a window into the watery underworld. Like the East Court, the West Court could easily have been flooded by the Maya, thus bringing to life the illusion heralded by its artwork.

Tunnels

To document and interpret the archaeological cut that was created by the Copan river on the East side of the Acropolis and reconstruct the historical development of its architecture, a major program of archaeological tunneling was carried out from

1989 until 1997. The vast majority of the buried buildings found here had been leveled by the Maya themselves to create solid foundations for the new constructions that went up over them. This process of "renewal" of buildings is documented throughout the Maya area but the Copan Acropolis is by far and away the best studied example. Happily, in some cases the buildings about to be buried were preserved almost to perfection, retaining details as delicate as modeled plaster reliefs and paint. To allow visitors a glimpse of this marvelous underground world at Copan, two tunnel circuits, named "Rosalila" and "Jaguars", have been consolidated, improved, and made fairly comfortable for tourists.

Rosalila

The name "Rosalila", as well as those given to many of the other buildings from the Acropolis mentioned here, comes from a time-honored tradition in Maya archaeology in which the discoverer assigns them a nick-name, giving preference to the

REPLICA OF ROSALILA, SCULPTURE MUSEUM

names of colors and birds. In this specific case the name refers to two reddish hues in Spanish, "rosa" (rose) and "lila" (lilac), which were combined into a single "rosalila".

Rosalila Structure is dated to the middle of the 6th century and is the best-preserved example of monumental architecture found in the tunnels at Copan. Unlike nearly all of the other buildings found here, it was not destroyed by the ancient Maya. Instead, it was buried with great care and ceremony. Rosalila is a unique example of the vivid colors used by the ancient Maya on their buildings. The predominant color is red accompanied by details in bright green, yellow, and orange.

The building measures 18.5 by 12.5 meters, and the principal façade is on the west side. The temple is placed over a three-meter tall terraced pyramid, named "Azul." The pyramidal base is modest compared to others in Copan, which can reach up to 20 meters. Like all other temples constructed on the Acropolis' central axis, the main steps face west, the direction the Maya associated with the entrance to the otherworld, the world of the dead, and the place where the sun died daily.

REPLICA OF
ROSALILA
ROOM

The smooth plastered interior walls of the temple were covered with soot from the burning of incense and torches, not unlike the walls of many old churches in the Maya area today. These rooms also still retain red painted ornamental bands on the walls. Amazingly, traces still exist of the round wooden beams used to span and support the sidewalls of the vaults.

Inside the temple many artifacts were found that reflect religious practices. Among these were seven ceramic incense burners with charcoal still inside; two of these lay upon sculpted, stone jaguar pedestals. In addition two flint knives (for sacrifices) were found, along with nine stunning eccentric flints (ceremonial scepters) wrapped in the remnants of a deep blue bag, carved jade jewelry, lustrous sea shells, sharp stingray spines (perforators for blood-letting rites), shark vertebrae and jaguar claws from necklaces, and the traces of flower petals and pine needles. Some of these remains (particularly the incense burners and the flowers) recall religious practices still in use among the living Maya.

Rosalila was the principal religious sanctuary at Copan in the late 6th century AD. It is the most completely preserved example of the art and architecture of this period discovered to date. Like the cover of an illuminated manuscript, the façades are elaborately decorated with complex religious messages. The themes are cosmological and emphasize the Sun God, K'inich Ahau, divine patron for Maya kings and the spiritual namesake of the Founder of the dynasty, K'inich Yax K'uk' Mo'. In fact, the Founder's name is interwoven with the images of the god on the artwork of the first level of the building.

The second level of the building is dominated by the masks of a witz monster, which marks Rosalila as a sacred mountain and the birthplace of maize, while the third level is dominated by a smoking skull that represents an incense burner. In this way, the building is also marked as a "house of smoke" or a "temple". In its heyday, this marvelous building was a showy religious shrine from which emanated colors, sounds, and odors as rich as those found today in the churches of highland Guatemala. Inside, copal burned continuously, flowers and pine needles carpeted the floor, and ritual chants reverberated from its walls.

The Rosalila Tunnel that is open to visitors goes in to the north side of the temple at the height of the upper half

1. ENTRANCE ROSALILA TUNNEL
2. NORTH FACADE MASK
3. NORTHWEST CORNER

of the first floor. There are two glass windows in the tunnel that allow you a view of the temple. The first one looks directly into the central image of the building which consists of a portrait of the Sun God, K'inich Ahau. To the left and right, all along the face of the temple, are the rest of the elaborate decorations that accompany this panel. The next window allows you the broadest view of Rosalila that can be had. The visitor stands next to the northwest corner of the building and from here on his left he can look back on the Sun God mask that he saw in the first window, while on his right is the western (and principal) façade of the building. Starting with its discovery on June 23rd, 1989, it took over four years of excavation to expose the area that is now visible at a glimpse in this window. Other tunnels, not open to the visitor, explored the small pyramid that served as a base for Rosalila, as well as the other two stories of the temple. The bright colors that decorate these façades are not evident from these windows because of the thick coat of white plaster that was placed on them when Rosalila was ceremoniously embalmed for its burial at the end of the 7th century AD. Nevertheless, careful observation will allow you to see traces of the colors in different areas where the white coat has been carefully removed to document the colors to be used in the replica of Rosalila in the Sculpture Museum.

Sub-Jaguar Tunnel

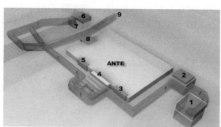

1. ENTRANCE 2. GALINDO TOMB 3. ANTE
MASK 01 4. HIEROGLYPHIC STEP ON ANTE
5. ANTE MASK 02 6. ANCIENT BATHROOM
7. EXIT TO EAST COURT 8. ANTE MASK 03
9. EXIT TO ARCHAEOLOGICAL CUT

As the visitor steps down into this tunnel from the East Court, the first exhibit he comes across is the "Galindo Tomb". This is a good example of what a royal tomb looks like at Copan. The fully dressed body would have been placed face-up on the floor of the tomb. On its sides, as well as in the four niches on the side walls would have been placed many of his personal items, including plates, cups, clothing, and jewelry. Many of these would have been full of food to accompany the deceased on his journey to the underworld. This tomb was excavated in 1834 by Colonel Juan Galindo. From his brief reports we know a little about the painted ceramic pots and shell necklaces that he found here but not much more. Galindo's Tomb was built against a beautiful edifice discovered in 1989 and named "Ante". Because of its location, it is believed that this tomb might have been the burial chamber for the 10th ruler of Copan.

The Sub-Jaguar Tunnel traces the outline of Ante Structure, running along its south, west and north sides. The western side is dominated by a central staircase with a hieroglyphic inscription on its sixth step. This inscription suggests that Ante was built by the 8th ruler around AD 540. On all three sides of the building, and particularly visible next to the stairway, are

BIRD MASK ON ANTE

beautiful plaster-modeled panels portraying sacred birds, avian creatures frequently associated with the divine at Copan. This artwork, along with other archaeological data, makes it evident that this building was contemporary with Rosalila.

Further along this tunnel are some interesting sanitary and hydraulic features. The first one of these is a wash basin built into the floor of the front room of a small building called "Cisne". It is the only one of its kind in Copan. This basin drains into a larger system of aqueducts that also channeled rainwater from the plazas in front of Cisne and Ante. The entry to part of this can be seen at the bottom of the stairs that lead down from Cisne. More sections of these drainages can be seen as one reaches the end of this tunnel circuit and sees daylight again.

ARCHAEOLOGY AND HISTORY AT COPAN

Monuments and Rulers

In the past few decades, advances in the decipherment of Maya hieroglyphs have been astounding. The resulting historical information has given us some great new insights into the lives of the rulers. We can now assign dates to the accession and death of many of them and thus define the outline of the dynastic history of the site.

The phonetic decipherment of the Maya script is a very recent, dynamic and ongoing process. There is still much to learn about these texts, and their information is limited in many aspects. They do not present the daily life of farmers, merchants, weavers, and artists. Rather they speak mostly about the activities of the kings and their courts.

ALTAR Q: NORTH SIDE

WEST SIDE

6   5   4   3   2   1   16   15

In the charts that follow, we present a summary of the time-lines that have resulted from the most recent work that provides the principal framework for reconstructing the dynastic history of this site.

Altar Q and the Late Rulers

 On the south side of Altar Q, below the second figure from the left, appears the hieroglyph that refers to the ruler nicknamed "18 Rabbit". It occupies the thirteenth position on the altar. He is the dominant figure on the stelae of the Great Plaza (A, B, C, D, F, H, and 4). On Stela B his name is associated with a glyph that signifies "13th in the succession", confirming his correct position on the altar.

DETAILS OF ALTAR Q: THE NUMBERS REFER TO THE SUCCESSION OF RULERS AT COPAN, AS SHOWN ON THE SIDES OF ALTAR Q.

ALL 16 MONARCHS OF THE DYNASTY ARE REPRESENTED. ON THE SOUTH SIDE OF THE ALTAR, THE FIRST RULER SYMBOLICALLY PRESENTS HIS SCEPTOR TO THE 16TH RULER.

SOUTH SIDE   EAST SIDE

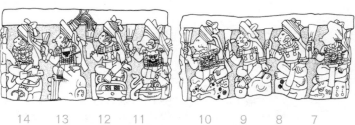

14   13   12   11   10   9   8   7

COPAN'S DYNASTY

NAME		YEARS IN POWER MONUMENTS
Kinich Yax Kuk' Mo' Great-Sun First Quetzal Macaw	1	426 - 437 A.D. *(8.19.10.0.0 - 9.0.2.0.0)* Motmot Marker Structures: Hunal, Yax, & Motmot
Kinich Popol Hol Mat Head	2	c. 437 - 470 A.D. *(9.0.2.0.0 - ?)* Stelas: 18 & 63; Xukpi Stone; Structures: Yehnal, Margarita, Papagayo & Mascarones
Unknown	3	c. 470 - 485 A.D. *(? - 9.2.10.0.0)*
Ku Ix (Cu Ix)	4	485 - 495 A.D. *(9.2.10.0.0 - 9.3.0.0.0)* Stela 34; Bench of Papagayo
Unknown	5	c. 500 - 510 A.D.
Unknown	6	c. 510 - 524 A.D.
Balam Nehn Waterlily Jaguar	7	524 - 532 A.D. *(9.4.10.0.0 - c. 9.4.18.6.12)* Stela 15
Wil Ohl Kinich	8	532 - 551 A.D. *(9.4.18.6.12 - 9.5.17.13.7)* Ante Step & Rosalila Step?
Sak Lu	9	551 - 553 A.D. *(9.5.17.13.7 - c. 9.5.19.3.0)* Altar X

Moon Jaguar 10   553 - 578 A.D.
(9.5.19.3.0 - 9.7.4.17.4)
Stelae 9 & 17; Rosalila Step?

Butz' Chan 11   578 - 628 A.D.
Smoke Serpent   *(9.7.5.0.8 - 9.9.14.16.9)*
Smoke Sky   Stelae P & 7; Altar Y

Smoke Jaguar 12   628 - 695 A.D.
Smoke Imix God K   *(9.9.14.17.5 - 9.13.3.5.9)*
Stelae I, 1, 2, 3, 5, 6, 10, 12,
13, 19 & 23; Altars H', I', K & 5;
Structure Chorcha

Waxaklajun Ub'ah K'awil 13   695 - 738 A.D.
18 Rabbit   *(9.13.3.6.8 - 9.15.6.14.6)*
Stelae A, B, C, D, F, H, J, and
4; Altar S; Structures 2, 4, 9,
10, 22, Esmeralda & Lower
Section of Hieroglyphic
Stairway; Ballcourts II-B & A-III;
Sun Court

K'ak'Joplaj Chan K'awil 14   738 - 749 A.D.
Smoke Monkey   *(9.15.6.16.5 - 9.15.17.12.16)*
Structure 22-A (Popol Na)

K'ak' Yipyaj Chan K'awil 15   749 - 763 A.D.
Smoke Shell   *(9.15.17.13.10 - c. 9.16.12.5.17)*
Squirrel   Stelae M & N; Upper Section of
the Hieroglyphic Stairway

Yax Pasaj Chan Yoaat 16   763 - before 820 A.D.
Yax Pac   *(9.16.12.5.17 - 9.19.10.0.0)*
Dawn   Stelae 8, 11 & 29; Altars G1,
G2, G3, O, Q, R, T, U, V, Z, B',
C', D', F', G', W', & 41; Struc-
tures 11, 16, 18, 21-A, 29 & 32.

Ukit Took' 17   Feb. 10, 822 - ? A.D.
U Cit Tok'   *(9.19.11.14.5 - ?)*
Final Pretender to the Throne
Altar L

Dates of Inscribed Monuments

Monument	Maya Calendar	Christian Calendar	Ruler
Stela 35		ca. AD 400	1
Motmot Marker	9.0.0.0.0	AD 435	1 & 2
Xukpi Stone	9.0.2.0.0	AD 437	2
Stela 63	ca. 9.1.10.0.0	ca. AD 465	2
Bench of Papagayo Structure	ca. 9.2.10.0.0	ca. AD 485	4
Stela 15	9.4.10.0.0	AD 524	7
Step/Ante	9.5.7.12.2	AD 542	8
Altar X	9.5.19.12.18	AD 553	10
Stela 9	9.6.10.0.0	AD 564	10
Step/Rosalila	9.6.17.3.2?	AD 571?	10 (?)
Stela 7	9.9.0.0.0	AD 613	11
Stela P	9.9.10.0.0	AD 623	11
Altar Y	9.9.14.17.5	AD 628	11
Stela 23	9.10.18.12.8	AD 651	12
Stela 3	9.10.19.5.0	AD 652	12
Stela 10	9.10.19.13.0	AD 652	12
Stela 19	9.10.19.15.0	AD 652	12
Stela 2	9.11.0.0.0	AD 652	12
Stela 12	9.11.0.0.0	AD 652	12
Stela 13	9.11.0.0.0	AD 652	12
Stela 5	9.11.15.0.0	AD 667	12
Stela 1	9.11.15.14.0	AD 668	12
Stela I	9.12.3.14.0	AD 675	12
Step, Structure 2	9.12.5.0.0	AD 677	12
Altar H'	9.12.8.3.10	AD 680	12
Stela 6	9.12.10.0.0	AD 682	12
Altar I'	9.12.10.0.0	AD 682	12
Altar K	9.12.16.7.8	AD 688	12
Stela E	?	?	12
Stela J	9.13.10.0.0	AD 702	13
Temple 22	9.14.3.6.8	AD 715	13
Stela F	9.14.10.0.0	AD 721	13

Monument	Maya Calendar	Christian Calendar	Ruler
Hiero. Stairway I	9.14.12.0.0	AD 723	13
Stela 4	9.14.15.0.0	AD 726	13
Stela H	9.14.19.5.0	AD 730	13
Stela C	9.14.19.5.0	AD 730	13
Stela A	9.14.19.8.0	AD 731	13
Stela B	9.15.0.0.0	AD 731	13
Altar S	9.15.0.0.0	AD 731	13
Stela D	9.15.5.0.0	AD 736	13
Ball Court III	9.15.6.8.13	AD 738	13
Structure 22-A	9.15.15.0.0	AD 746	14
Hiero.Stairway II	9.16.4.1.0	AD 755	15
Stela M	9.16.5.0.0	AD 756	15
Stela N	9.16.10.0.0	AD 761	15
Altar F'	9.16.13.12.1	AD 764	16
Altar G3	9.16.15.0.0	AD 766	16
Temple 11	9.16.18.2.12	AD 769	16
Altar Z	9.16.18.9.19	AD 769	16
Altar V	9.17.0.0.0	AD 771	16
Altar D'	9.17.0.0.0	AD 771	16
Structure 21-A	9.17.0.0.0	AD 771	16
Altar Q	9.17.5.3.4	AD 776	16
Altar W'	9.17.5.9.4	AD 776	16
Structure 9M-158	9.17.6.17.7	AD 777	16
Structure 9N-82	9.17.10.11.0	AD 781	16
Altar T	9.17.12.5.17	AD 783	16
Stela 8	9.17.12.6.2	AD 783	16
Altar U	9.18.1.13.2	AD 792	16
Altar R	9.18.2.8.0	AD 792	16
Altar G2	9.18.5.0.0	AD 795	16
Altar G1	9.18.10.0.0	AD 800	16
Temple 18	9.18.10.17.18	AD 801	16
Stela 11	9. 19. 10.0.0	AD 820	16
Altar L	9.19.11.14.5	AD 822	Final Pretender?

STELA 4

STELA A

STELA D

STELAE IN THE SUN COURT. ALL WERE COMMISSIONED BY 18 RABBIT.

STELA H AND ITS ALTAR

The 13th Ruler's name is composed of a number (consisting of three bars, each with a numerical value of five, and three dots, each with a value of one, thus representing the number 18) above an animal head. Some epigraphers have interpreted this head as that of a "rabbit", giving room to his popular nickname. On the right is the head of the god K'awil. The prevalent translation of his name today is "Waxaklahun Ub'ah K'awil", which means "18 are the images of the God K'awil", this lightning god being one of the primary deities associated with Maya royalty.

Among the great achievements of the thirteenth ruler was the transition of Copan's free-standing sculptures from relatively low relief to the high relief, nearly full-round style for which Copan is now justly famous. Under his leadership, the Great Plaza was given its present form. He is also responsible for the final version of the Ball Court, the first construction of the Hieroglyphic Stairway of Structure 26, and the ornate Temple 22 of the Acropolis. He has been referred to as the "King of the Arts" of ancient Copan.

18 RABBIT, STELA B. (731 A.D.)

43

The following ruler (14th in the sequence) reigned for a relatively short and probably turbulent time (11 years), due to the dramatic fall of his predecessor. On May 3 A.D. 738, the 13th Ruler was captured and decapitated by the ruler of Quiriguá. This Maya center had originally been a part of the Copan Kingdom. The triumph was widely heralded at Quiriguá, where the ruler proceeded to erect some of the tallest stelae in the Maya area. In Copan it was a time of duress; as a result, the 14th Ruler did not erect stelae of his own.

This ruler is known by the nickname "Smoke Monkey"; and on the base of Stela N (where he is associated with the glyph "14th in the succession"), he is

POPOL NAH

identified as the father of the next king. On Altar Q, his name glyph is found under the figure on the extreme left of the south side, which corresponds to the 14th position in the sequence

POPOL NAH, BUILT BY 14TH RULER IN 746 A.D.

44

THE FIRST PHASE OF THE HIEROGLYPHIC STAIRCASE WAS CON-
STRUCTED BY 18 RABBIT, THE 13TH RULER; IT WAS FINISHED BY
THE 15TH RULER, WHO WAS KNOWN AS "SMOKE MONKEY".

of rulers. Recent archaeological investigations have assigned
Structure 22-A to his reign. This building has been identified
by its sculpture as the Popol Nah or the Council House.

His son, the 15th Ruler, finished the second and final version
of the imposing Hieroglyphic Stairway, and Stelae M and N. The
glyphic elements of the main part of his name led to the nickname "Smoke Shell". His successor, Yax Pasaj, mentioned this
ruler often, as on the Reviewing Stand of Temple 11. The principal element of his name is found below the figure seated in
the 15th position, on the far right of the front side of Altar Q.

The Hieroglyphic Stairway, with more than 1,250 glyph blocks in its inscription, is a historical narrative which highlights the accomplishments of the ancestors of Smoke Shell. Written here are the names of earlier rulers and their major feats. The rulers were portrayed as seated figures along the middle of the stairway and on the roof crest of the temple above. They are shown bearing shields and other instruments of war. Some of the events narrated in the stairway text record battles and conquests by these rulers.

The name of the 16th ruler is found on dozens of monuments. His accession is heralded on the front part of Altar Q and on Temple 11. This ruler rebuilt a major part of the Acropolis, giving the form to many of the buildings that we see today. In looking at the texts that refer to his inauguration, it is evident that there were

LOW RELIEF PORTRAIT OF 16TH RULER, YAX PASAJ, ON TEMPLE 18

many ways that scribes wrote his name. The most widely accepted reading today is "Yax Pasaj", which can be translated as "First Dawn" or "Sunrise".

Yax Pasaj sponsored many kinds of inscribed monuments but is perhaps best known for the elaborate inscribed benches or thrones found in the residential areas of Copan as well as the Acropolis. Supporting the benches, almost invariably, are representations of Bacabs or Pauahtuns, who were the four Maya gods that sustained the sky and the earth.

The widespread use of façade sculpture was another art style perpetuated by Yax Pasaj. This gave Copan a distinctive, magisterial quality, adding to its great artistic luster.

Earlier Rulers

Information about many of the early rulers is hard to find, due in large part to the Maya custom of destroying and burying buildings and monuments in the constant quest to renew the world and its sacred order. Nevertheless, archaeological research is giving us more and more insights each day, as we probe into the earlier buildings, buried deep beneath the final buildings that we admire on the surface of the site today.

On Stela 6, erected in A.D. 681, the 12th Ruler known as "Smoke Jaguar" or "Smoke Imix God K" is mentioned along with his heir, "18 Rabbit," who was to accede to the throne some 14 years later. Smoke Jaguar was extremely powerful and long-lived, ruling from A.D. 628 until 695. During his lifetime he erected more than ten stelae, at least five altars with hieroglyphic inscriptions, and two architectural inscriptions. He also set his stone sculptors to carving architectural façades with very high relief figural art, breaking away from earlier traditions of modeled plaster. He lived to be an octogenarian, which explains why in the 12th position on Altar Q he is referred to simply as a "5 katun lord". Thus the fact that Smoke Jaguar had entered his fifth katun (fifth 20-year period) was highlighted. His long reign and great accomplishments were also celebrated on the first version of the Hieroglyphic Stairway on Structure 26.

PORTRAIT OF 12TH RULER, SMOKE JAGUAR, ON STELA 6, (CAN BE SEEN ON THE HIGHWAY BETWEEN THE PARK AND THE TOWN.)

One of the great ironies of history is that in the year A.D. 652 Smoke Jaguar was recorded on Altar L of Quiriguá, as patron for the new ruler

47

of this town. Eighty-six years later, the descendants of this ruler would capture and decapitate Smoke Jaguar's son, 18 Rabbit.

The predecessor of Smoke Jaguar is called "Butz´ Chan", which can be translated as "Smoke Serpent" or "Smoke Sky" ("Chan" in Mayan means both "serpent" and "sky"). He was another of the great rulers of Copan, assuming kingship at the tender age of 15, and remaining in power until his death 49 years later on January 23 A.D. 628. His reign, when combined with that of the 12th and 13th rulers, covered some 160 years (A.D. 578-738) of the dynastic history of Copan. This was the greatest era of demographic, political, social, and artistic growth in the city's history. The longevity of these reigns brought the stability which was necessary for this growth. After them, only Yax Pasaj, at the end of the city's history, had a reign of similar length (57 years).

Only two stelae (7 and P) are know to date to the reign of Butz' Chan. Stela 7 originally formed part of a large architectural complex located where the town of Copan Ruinas stands today. It is on display at the Anthropology Museum in the village's main square, not far from its place of origin. Stela P, on the other hand, is found in the West Court of the Acropolis, very close to Altar Q.

The tenth ruler—who is one of the candidates for building Rosalila—is known by the name "Moon Jaguar" and was in power from A.D. 553 to 578. One of the monuments known from his reign was found in the modern village, highlighting once again the importance of this locality for several of the Copan

STELA P, 623 A.D.

48

kings. Stela 9 tells us that Moon Jaguar was the son of "Waterlily Jaguar", the seventh in the line of dynastic succession from the founder.

Between the reigns of these two kings are two brothers (the 8th and the 9th rulers) who are little known. Their two reigns lasted a total of only nine years. It seems likely that they were either the younger brothers of Waterlily Jaguar, or perhaps his sons. In any case, both men seem to have died shortly after assuming the throne. A royal tomb recently discovered below the platform of the jaguars in the East Court of the Acropolis may well be that of Waterlily Jaguar.

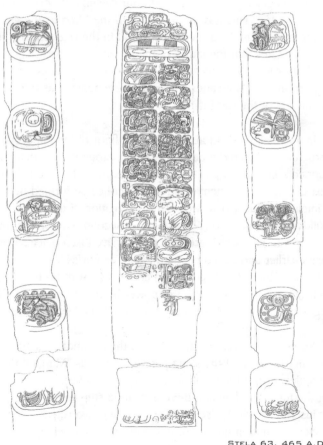

STELA 63, 465 A.D.

49

The third, fifth and sixth rulers are also practically unknown, whereas tales of the second and fourth are beginning to emerge from the rubble. This has come about through the discovery of carved monuments recently unearthed inside the Temple of the Hieroglyphic Stairway, in a buried temple which has been given the nickname, "Papagayo". Both the second and fourth rulers dedicated inscribed monuments inside Papagayo.

Stela 63 records a very important anniversary, the "Period Ending" of 9.0.0.0.0 of the Maya calendar. This signals the completion of the eighth cycle, or baktun (400-year period), and the beginning of the ninth. In our calendar it corresponds to A.D. 435. This was as significant to the Maya as the change of the millennium to the Western world in the year 2000. Stela 63 also states that the father of the second ruler was "K'inich Yax K'uk' Mo'. With his father he presided over the period-ending ceremony. Thereafter, his father is recognized as the "Founder" of the royal dynasty of Copan.

In 1993, investigations beneath the floor of the Papagayo Structure uncovered a beautiful circular stone marker that capped a cylindrical pit, full of rich offerings. The hieroglyphic text on the marker mentions a deer sacrifice performed by K'inich Yax K'uk' Mo' as well as his dedication of an adjacent building, "Motmot", on 9.0.0.0.0. A second date on the marker refers to acts which are believed to have taken place seven years earlier and would be cited again, centuries later, on top of Altar Q. Ruler 2 is also cited in connection with both events, indicating that the transition of power from the Founder to his legitimate son was of great concern to K'inich Yax K'uk' Mo'.

Some 100 meters to the south of the Motmot Structure is another building of the same period, known as "Margarita". It contains a royal tomb with unprecedented riches. To one side of the funerary chamber, there is a stone step with a hieroglyphic inscription which also mentions the first two rulers. The skeleton found in the tomb, however, does not belong to a man but to a prominent lady whose death chamber was opened up and revisited on a number of occasions by subsequent generations. The archaeologists responsible for these investigations speculate that they could be the remains of the wife of K'inich' Yax K'uk' Mo', mother of the 2nd Ruler.

Underneath Margarita there are two even more ancient buildings, one of which (called "Hunal") contains another elaborate royal tomb. The studies of this tomb suggest that it is the funerary chamber of the Founder of the city, K'inich Yax K'uk' Mo'. He is the central figure on Altar Q who passes the staff of office to Yax Pasaj. He is the first in the line of legitimate rulers, and the one who sanctions the right of all others to occupy the throne.

Recent Archaeological Investigations

With the intensive archaeological investigations carried out under the auspices of the government of Honduras since 1975, it has been possible to demonstrate that the growth of Copan was gradual. The incorporation of diverse families into a unified society under the rule of a single royal family apparently coincided with the introduction of hieroglyphic writing and the reign of K'inich Yax K'uk' Mo' around the beginning of the fifth century A.D.

Both the royal lineage and the art style prospered and flourished for some four centuries. The city grew progressively in size and diversity through time, culminating in a state that controlled a vast territory.

To find out more about both the collapse of the center and the demographic growth that preceded it, the archaeological projects in Copan began by studying the ecological setting, the carrying capacity of the restricted alluvial valley in which Copan is situated, and the number, form, and function of the ancient settlements that were found within its limits.

The investigations into the agricultural potential and use of the valley indicate that in its final decades, Copan was not self-sufficient in agriculture, and as a consequence found itself dependent upon foodstuffs brought in from neighboring valleys. The systematic recording of all of the ruins of rural Pre-Columbian settlements, plotted in detail on scaled maps, confirms a great density of population.

In the 24 square kilometers that surround the Principal Group, the remains of 3,450 surface structures have been located, of which more than 1,000 are found in the urban nucleus of two square kilometers surrounding the Acropolis. At present, archaeologists have expanded the systematic site survey to an area of 135 square kilometers, extending out from the Principal Group all the way to the natural geographic limits of what was the primary zone of power and influence for Copan. In this region they have detected some 1,425 sites with 4,507 structures. Updated population estimates indicate that during the 8th century A.D., at the time of peak population, the city of Copan had over 27,500 inhabitants, a figure not to be reached again until the 1980s.

1-2. PRINCIPAL GROUP   3. EL BOSQUE   4. LAS SEPULTURAS

The maps of the residential sites in the urban nucleus permitted the definition of two large wards or "barrios": one to the northeast which is presently called "Las Sepulturas" (the Sepulchres), and another to the southwest known as "El Bosque" (the Forest). Both designations correspond to the traditional names given by the modern inhabitants of the area. In both wards plaster-paved roads (sacbes) were found. These originated in the Principal Group and served as the primary avenues of access to the political, social and religious center of the ancient metropolis. The different kinds of architecture found in the residential compounds within the wards suggest marked differences in social class and prestige among their respective occupants.

In 1976 the Harvard Copan Valley Project dug three different residential sites, thought to represent three social strata, in the residential area east of the Principal Group. Beginning in December, 1980, an ambitious program of excavations and restoration was initiated in Las Sepulturas. This project was designed to resolve questions about the social structure of the ancient Maya community and at the same time restore dozens of ancient buildings and leave them accessible to visitors.

The investigations spanned the spectrum from the homes of the humblest field hands to the imposing palaces of the Great Plaza. In addition, the scrutiny of the ancient kingdom extended beyond the limits of the Copan Valley, in order to establish how far its hegemony extended.

In terms of the history of the ancient city, the study of ceramics found in the Copan Valley shows that the first sedentary village agriculturalists lived here around 1400 B.C. Their successors continued to produce various kinds of ceramic vessels until the end of the Classic Period, around the year A.D. 850, when their tracks gradually fade away. The principal period of architectural activity in the city fell between the years A.D. 400 and 820, when the royal dynasty was in its heyday.

Las Sepulturas

1. LAS SEPULTURAS 2. THE PRINCIPAL GROUP

COURTYARD IN LAS SEPULTURAS

 Las Sepulturas is the residential ward located to the northeast of the Principal Group. It consists of approximately 40 residential compounds. Of these, some 18 have been investigated, representing nearly 100 buildings with more than 200 rooms, which makes this the most complete excavated sample of urban domestic architecture of the ancient Maya. The selected residential compounds seem to reflect accurately the existence of at least four social classes, grouped from the poorest to the richest.

The residential group selected for the purpose of investigating the upper class (9N-8) was found to contain sophisticated and complex architecture, including masonry buildings with corbelled vaults, and one of the longest occupation sequences in the valley–nearly 2000 years of history in a single locus.

The excavations began with the largest buildings of the group, known as Structure 9N-82, or the Palace of the Scribe, where an exquisite sculptured bench was discovered, which is now on display in the Regional Museum of Copan Ruinas. The bench was carved in A.D. 781 and dedicated to an individual suspected of being an important scribe and "keeper of sacred things" in the royal court of the 16th ruler of Copan, Yax Pasaj.

CELESTIAL BENCH FROM LAS SEPULTURAS

His palace, the main part of which is restored in the Sculpture Museum, is a stone block building with a corbelled vault and an elaborate sculpture façade. It is believed that the majority of the rooms next to the main quarters, which mark the limits of a very private rectangular patio, were used as lodgings for the wives and offspring of the patriarch. The 16th century Spanish chroniclers noted that polygamy was firmly established among the upper classes of Maya society. This supposition is confirmed by the large burial sample from Las Sepulturas (more than 250), in which there are a disproportionate number of females, as one would expect in a polygamous society.

The excavations in this site revealed a series of other residential buildings constructed around small rectangular patios that were added onto those of the lord. Historical analogy with Maya groups of the Colonial Period leads us to believe that

SCRIBE'S PALACE, REBUILT IN THE SCULPTURE MUSEUM

these patios were probably home to the older sons of the nobles, their respective families, and their servants.

Some constructions had specialized functions. A case in point is that of a building found close to the Palace of the Scribe, containing a large quantity of ritual objects related to the ballgame. This structure was probably used as headquarters for a team of ballplayers in the service of the head of this residential compound.

The presence of fragments of shell, needles, awls, and drills on the floors of the patios between the buildings of another compound implies that the specialty of this group was the manufacture of shell goods and the preparation of textiles, leather goods, or baskets. It is possible that this was a group of artisans assigned to the court of a renowned Maya scribe.

BENCH IN SCRIBE'S PALACE

FACADE, SCRIBE'S PALACE

RUINS OF THE SCRIBE'S PALACE, IN LAS SEPULTURAS

Also found in the residential compounds in Las Sepulturas were numerous trash heaps containing the waste products of the daily life of their occupants: ceramic pots and pans, jars, plates, and cups that were used for storing, preparing and serving food; grinding stones used to process maize kernels into dough for making tortillas, tamales, and other foods; knives made of obsidian or volcanic glass, used for cutting and food processing (e.g., skinning and butchering animals); and occasionally the actual remains of the foodstuffs themselves. This has allowed us to know that their favorite vegetables and fruits included maize, beans, pumpkin, squash, avocadoes and nance fruit while their favorite animal food included white-tail deer, pocket gopher, peccary (wild boar), armadillo, parrots, fish and freshwater snails.

Among the numerous burials discovered around the buildings, and frequently inside them, two stand out. One is that of an aged healer or shaman who lived around A.D. 450, and the other, that of a child burial dating to about 900 B.C. The latter contained hundreds of pieces of well carved and highly polished jade, as well as sumptuous ceramic offerings which show participation in the trade and religious system led by the mysterious Olmec, founders of the first civilization of Mesoamerica over a millennium before Christ.

The architecture and ceramics of the early remains found in the investigations of Las Sepulturas and other areas of the valley have led most specialists to conclude that the majority of the valley population had its roots among the Lenca linguistic and ethnic group. From the beginning, Copan was a major exchange center in the southeastern frontier of Mesoamerica. Rich and diverse cultural and ecological networks led to the flourishing of a truly multi-ethnic city, a splendorous and cosmopolitan urban center on the edge of the Maya world.

The explorations in Las Sepulturas have given us a new perspective on the evolution of Maya domestic compounds, the composition of the social groups that resided in them, and the daily economic, social, political, and religious activities that were carried out in them. The wealth of information obtained through intensive excavations has provided an ever more detailed understanding of the daily life of the people of Copan.

TOMB IN LAS SEPULTURAS

The Principal Group

With the insights into the social, political, and economic life of the ancient "Copanecos" (people from Copan) provided by the work in the Copan Valley, archaeologists have returned to work in the Principal Group with a more comprehensive scientific and historical focus than that of their predecessors of years gone by. Even more important, they have returned to the heart of the kingdom for the purpose of conserving the most grandiose vestiges of the ancient city and its extraordinary architecture and sculpture.

Using excavation and restoration techniques developed in Las Sepulturas, researchers have gone back to study the buildings excavated by archaeological expeditions of the late 19th and early 20th century, with excellent results. A primary task has

59

been the sorting, cataloguing, study, and conservation of 28,000 fragments of sculpture fallen from the building façades and previously scattered throughout the site. The vast majority have now been successfully assigned to the buildings they originally adorned. The detailed study of their design motifs allow us, at the same time, to identify the purpose of those structures, as well as the name of the kings who commissioned them.

Although it may not seem this way to the first-time visitor, the majority of the sculpture carved in Copan is not to be found in the stelae and altars which have given Copan its wide acclaim, but in the architectural façades. This becomes evident when visiting the Sculpture Museum in Copan, inaugurated in 1996, where the exquisite façades of eight of these buildings have been reconstructed. Thus, the museum gives new life to the splendor of this ancient Maya metropolis.

SCULPTED THRONE IN THE INTERIOR CHAMBER OF TEMPLE 22

The work carried out with mosaic sculpture allows us to know that both Temple 26 (with the Hieroglyphic Stairway) and Temple 16 (in the uppermost central part of the Acropolis), were dedicated to war, death, and the worship of royal ancestors (particularly deceased kings); that Temple 118 was the Funerary Temple of Yax Pasaj, who is exalted as a warrior on the sculptures carved in its walls; that Temple 22 was a "Sacred Mountain", the site of rituals and sacrifices by the kings who performed their official duties surrounded by symbols of the entire Maya cosmos; and that Structure 22-A, the "Popol Nah", was the "Council House" or "Community House" where the kings met with their principal advisers to make the critical decisions that would determine the destiny of the state.

On the other hand, by excavating tunnels into the interior of the pyramids that served as the bases for the final generation of palaces and temples, it has been possible to search for the early roots of the city and its historical development. Most of the buildings and their respective substructures were destroyed by the Maya to cover them with new constructions. In other cases, they were conserved almost to perfection, retaining delicate features such as the stucco sculptures on their façades, with details of color and nuance still intact.

In this search for knowledge, archaeologists have excavated their way into three kilometers of tunnels under the Acropolis. For the monument's security, many of the tunnels have been sealed again after recording the necessary data; others have been kept open to allow access to scholars and conservation staff. A few have been consolidated to help the visitor get a better picture of the beauties still unearthed in Copan. The richness of this information complements that which was obtained in the valley to give us a more accurate global vision of the rulers, and the ruled, in the ancient Maya kingdom of Copan.

The Collapse

Archaeological investigations indicate that during its final decades, the city of Copan saw an unprecedented demographic growth. This brought with it a great intensification of the agricultural system, which in turn caused a spiraling rate of environmental degradation.

The expanding population was forced to spread into areas that were hardly apt for settlement, let alone agriculture, on the steep slopes of the hills and mountains that surrounded the valley. There they deforested wide areas, which were already only sparsely covered with trees due to the demands for wood for construction and more particularly for firewood for food preparation, light in the homes at night, and the production of lime for plaster floors and building façades. Samples obtained by paleoecologists provide evidence of this process.

Similarly, archaeologists working in the valley have found indications of massive erosion of the soils in the foothills and mountains. It is also believed that there were marked climatic changes: intense droughts, with river and stream levels going even lower, disastrous floods during the rainy season caused by the lack of vegetation cover to slow down the flow, etc.

The impact on the human population was equally severe. Specialists in charge of the study of the skeletal remains (physical anthropologists)—who in Copan have the largest sample in the Maya region—have found marked evidence of malnutrition, infectious diseases, and traumatic growth. Life expectancy decreased through time until, at the end, many children between the ages of five and fifteen were dying, which is precisely the segment of the population that should be the most resilient.

A tragic symbol of the end of the kingdom is Altar L. In the year A.D. 822, a pretender to the throne named Ukit Took' commissioned this monument to honor his accession to power, in the same way that Yax Pasaj did on Altar Q. However the altar was never finished, the majority of its faces remaining uncarved. With this pathetic figure, who was not even able to finish proclaiming his reign, the powerful dynasty that started with K'inich Yax K'uk' Mo' drew to a close.

After the collapse of the monarchical government, the poverty-stricken population continued to inhabit the area around the Principal Group, but they slowly began to abandon the ecologically devastated Copan Valley. It is possible that as much as two centuries elapsed before the valley was completed abandoned, and the forest began the slow process of rebuilding the soils that man had abused and destroyed.

On the basis of the scientific investigations of the archaeological projects, our vision of the Copan Maya has changed dramatically: from a theocratic society to one with a more secular government; from one that spoke of vacant ceremonial centers, to that of a vibrant urban population center of about 28,000 inhabitants; from a group of temples to the palaces of the nobility; from sculptures of gods to those of rulers; from a writing of astronomy and divination to one of historical annals and naming of monuments, buildings, and portable objects. At the same time, with the enormous technological advances and new perspectives for study, every day we come to know this marvelous civilization in greater detail, making us more aware that there is still a great deal to be learned about the ancient Maya and their non-Maya neighbors.

ALTAR L
WAS NEVER FINISHED.

BIBLIOGRAPHY

Andrews, E. Wyllys and William L. Fash, eds.
    2005   *Copán: The History of an Ancient Maya Kingdom.*
           School of American Research Press. Santa Fe.

Agurcia Fasquelle, Ricardo
    1997   'Le temple du roi Soleil et son évolution au coeur de l'acropole de
           Copán'. In *Les Mayas au Pays de Copán*. pp. 91-100. Skira editore,
           Italy.

    1998   'Copán: Art, Science and Dynasty'. In *Maya*. P.Schmidt, M.de la
           Garza and E. Nalda, eds. pp. 336-355. Bompiani, Italy.

    2007   *Copán: Reino del Sol/ Kingdom of the Sun.*
           Editorial Transamérica, Tegucigalpa.

Agurcia Fasquelle, Ricardo and William L. Fash, Jr.
    1989   'Copán: A royal Maya Tomb Discovered'. *National
           Geographic Magazine*, 176(4):481-487.

    1991   'Maya Artistry Unearthed'. *National Geographic
           Magazine*, 180(3):94-105.

Agurcia F., Ricardo, Donna.K. Stone, and Jorge Ramos
    1996   'Tierra, tiestos, piedras, estratigrafía y escultura: Investigaciones en
           la Estructura 10L-16 de Copán'. *Visión del Pasado Maya*, edited by
           W.L. Fash and R. Agurcia F., pp. 185-201. Asociación Copán, Copán.

Agurcia F., Ricardo and Juan Antonio Valdés
    1994   *Secretos de Dos Ciudades Mayas/Secrets of Two Maya Cities:
           Copán y/& Tikal.* Centro Editorial, San Pedro Sula.

Baudez, Claude F., ed.
    1983   *Introducción a la Arqueologia de Copán, Honduras.* 3 vols.
           Secretaria de Estado en el Despacho de Cultura y Turismo.
           Tegucigalpa, Honduras

Bell, Ellen, Marcello Canuto and Robert Sharer
    2004   *Understanding Early Classic Copan.* Univ. of Pennsylvania Museum,
           Philadelphia.

Fash, Barbara
    1992   'Late Classic Architectural Sculpture Themes in Copán'. *Ancient
           Mesoamerica* 3:89-104.

Fash, William
    2001   *Scribes, Warriors, and Kings: The City of Copán and the Ancient
           Maya.* Thames and Hudson, London and New York.

Fash, William L. and Ricardo Agurcia Fasquelle
    1996   *Visión del Pasado Maya.* Centro Editorial, San Pedro Sula.

Martin, Simon and Nikolai Grube
    2000   *Chronicle of the Maya Kings and Queens.* Thames & Hudson, New York.

Maudslay, Alfred P.
    1889   *Biologia Centrali Americana: Archaeology.* Vol. 1. R.H. Porter and
           Dulau and Co., London.

Miller, Mary E.
   1986   'Copán Honduras: Conference with a Perished City'. In *City States of the Maya: Art and Architecture*, edited by E.P.Benson, pp. 72-108. Rocky Mountain Institute for Pre-Columbian Studies, Denver.

Morley, Sylvanus
   1920   *The Inscriptions at Copan*. Carnegie Institution of Washington, Washington, D.C.

Robicsek, Francis
   1972   *Copan: Home of the Mayan Gods*. Museum of the American Indian, New York.

Sanders, William T., ed.
   1986   *Excavaciones en el Area Urbana de Copan*. Instituto Hondureño de Antropología e Historia, Tegucigalpa, Honduras.

Schele, Linda and David Freidel
   1990   *A Forest of Kings: The Untold Story of the Classic Maya*. William Morrow and Co., Inc., New York.

Schele, Linda and Mary Ellen Miller.
   1986   *The Blood of Kings: Dynasty and Ritual in Maya Art*. Kimbell Art Museum, Fort Worth.

Sharer, Robert J. with Loa P. Traxler
   2006   *The Ancient Maya*. Sixth Edition. Stanford University Press, Stanford.

Stuart, George E.
   1989   'Copán: City of Kings and Commoners'. *National Geographic Magazine*, 176(4):488-505.

   1997   'The Royal Crypts of Copán'. *National Geographic Magazine*, 192(6):68-93.

Taube, Karl A.
   1992   *The Major Gods of Ancient Yucatan*. Dumbarton Oaks, Washington, D.C.

   1993   *Aztec and Maya Myths*. British Museum Press, Avon.

   2000   'The Turquoise Hearth: Fire, Self-Sacrifice, and the Central Mexican Cult of War'. In *Mesoamerica's Classic Heritage: From Teotihuacan to the Aztec*, edited by D. Carrasco, L. Jones, and S. Sessions, pp. 269-340. U. of Colorado Press, Niwot.

Webster, David
   1999   'The Archaeology of Copán, Honduras'. *Journal of Archaeological Research*, 7(1):1-53.

Webster, David, AnnCorinne Freter and Nancy Gonlin
   2000   *Copan: The Rise and Fall of an Ancient Maya Kingdom*. Wadsworth, Belmont.

Wisdom, Charles.
   1961   *Los Chortis de Guatemala*. Ministerio de Educación Pública, Guatemala.

The Copan Association

ASOCIACION
COPAN

WHO WE ARE:

The Copan Association is a Honduran non-profit organization founded in 1990 dedicated to the research and conservation of national heritage. Guided by leaders in Middle American research, the Copan Association has been directed since its creation by Ricardo Agurcia Fasquelle, Honduran archaeologist and community leader.

We promote and support

- Research, education and conservation of the cultural and natural heritage of Honduras
- Training for Hondurans in Anthropology and related fields
- Projects that promote intelligent stewardship of the cultural and natural landscape

Completed Projects

1. Rescue and Stabilization of the Acropolis River Cut
2. School Nurseries for Reforestation
3. More than five books on Copan
4. Investigation and Consolidation of Temple 16 (Rosalila & Oropendola Structures.)
5. The Sculpture Museum of Copan
6. The Casa K'inich Maya Learning Center
7. Management Plan for the archaeological site of Los Naranjos
8. Second and Third Copan International Conferences (2001, 2007) www.copancongress.com

Ongoing Projects

1. DIPA/PDRVC (Integrated Development of Archaeological Parks financed by the World Bank)
2. Expansion of the Casa K'inich Maya Learning Center
3. New publications